A Heart on Fire

ST. JOHN EUDES:
A Model for the
New Evangelization

Written by Steven S. Marshall

Edited by Fr. Eleuterio Mireles, Jr. CJM

Photos from Ri courtesy of Fr. Ernesto Torres CJM.
Cartoons by Alain d'Orange, from his illustrations of *Saint Jean Eudes,*
by Fr. Robert de Pas CJM, Paris: Éditions Fleurus, 1969,
First published without copyright, now in the public domain.

ISBN: 978-0-9979114-8-0

Copyright ©2018, by
The Eudists – Congregation of Jesus and Mary, US Region

All Rights Reserved.

Published by

EUDIST
PRESS

744 Sonrisa Street
Solana Beach, CA 92075
www.eudistsusa.org

THE
EUDISTS
CONGREGATION OF
JESUS AND MARY

Table of Contents

Introduction

A Heart on Fire

"I have come to set the world on fire, and
how I wish it was already burning"
— Luke 12:49

Fire. *"I want to run to Paris, through the halls of the Sorbonne and other
universities, crying out 'Fire! Fire! The fires of hell engulf the whole world!*

*Come, esteemed doctors, come holy fathers and clergy, help us extin-
guish this fire!...Souls perish by the thousands for lack of those willing to
reach out to them."* [1]

These are the words of St. John Eudes, a missionary to those most in
need of mercy, an evangelist to fallen-away Catholics and an educator of
priests. He is often portrayed with a heart on fire in his hand, because his
life was driven by a burning love for the people of God.

In fact, he was a simple man from humble beginnings. How did he
become a saint? What does his life as a missionary mean for us today?

Chapter One

An Adorer of Truth

"You will know the truth, and the Truth
will set you free."

— John 8:32

John Eudes started his life of faith just like the rest of us: in the waters of
baptism. In 1601, he was born in Ri, a tiny hamlet in Normandy, France.
His birth, however, was an answer to prayer. In his autobiography, John
tells us:

*"My father and mother were married three years without being able to
have children because of a curse that had been put upon them. Then they
made a pilgrimage in honor of the Blessed Virgin, going to the shrine of
Notre Dame de la Recouvrance... Afterward, my mother then being preg-
nant, she and my father returned to that same chapel where they offered
and consecrated me to Our Lord and Our Lady."* [2]

SEPTEMBRE 1853
NOUS SOMMES TROIS FRÈRES ADORATEURS DE LA VÉRITÉ
L'AINÉ LA PRÊCHE LE CADET L'ÉCRIT
ET MOI JE LA DÉFENDRAI JUSQU'A MON DERNIER SOUPIR

At this point in history, witch-hunts were commonplace, and people ordinarily believed in curses, especially in rural villages. What was surprising was the answer to the parents' prayer. John was the first of seven children and the three boys all became famous for their deeds. A plaque on a memorial in Ri quotes John's youngest brother, who said:

"We three brothers are Adorers of Truth. The oldest preached it, the next wrote it, and I, I will defend it until my last breath"

John became famous for the missions he preached, similar to today's Billy Graham. Francois, the middle brother became a royal historian and a member of the famous Academie Francaise. Charles, the next in line, became a town magistrate, and was well-known for his high moral standards.

Each one of us begins our life of faith with a certain heritage. John's father, Isaac Eudes, was a hard-working farmer and the village doctor. He taught his boys to know what is right, to face reality, and to be persistent in doing what needs to be done. From an early age, John connected this attitude with Scripture. Once, while playing with other children in town, another boy slapped him on the cheek. John's response was to turn the other cheek. He had heard the phrase from the Bible, so in childlike faith, he let the truth affect his actions.

Not all of our childhood influences are positive, though. In reflecting on his life, John describes his parish as a place where Catholicism was cultural, at best: *"There was very little instruction for salvation, and very few people ever received communion except during the Easter season. Me, I began to know God when I was about twelve years old through a very special grace of His divine goodness, and to receive communion every month after making a general confession."*[3]

In fact, neither parish catechism classes or regular reception of the Eucharist were commonly practiced in France at this time. Up until the Edict of Nantes, signed in 1598 (just three years before John's birth), the law was "cuius regio, eius religio," meaning that citizens were required to simply accept the religion of their king. Catholicism often became a political affiliation, and its rites were often reduced to routine or superstition. In short, virtually everyone born was baptized, but very few were taught the miracle of what takes place in the sacraments.

God, in His providence would later turn John into a missionary to teach the dignity and the obligations which are given to us in baptism. However, to reach that point, some help would be needed.

The first influence in John's life who showed him a faith different than the status quo was Madame de Sacy, the wife of the local baron, who owned a small mansion in Ri. Her Catholicism was different: it was exciting and active, and it sparked John's curiosity. She was part of a prayer group which gathered in Paris to read the works of the mystics, especially Theresa of Avila and John of the Cross.

The group was started by Cardinal de Berulle, who was a close friend of St. Francis de Sales. The group brought together faithful priests with Paris high-society, and was at the forefront of what was called a "spiritual invasion" in France. For John to have contact with this new wave of evangelization in a remote village of 200 people was surprising, to say the least, but it was the first of many turning points in his journey as an adorer of truth, and a tool in the hand of God.

Chapter Two
A Lover of Jesus and Mary

"I loved wisdom, and sought her from
my youth. I desired to take her for
my bride."

— Wisdom 8:2

At first, it was not the intention of John's parents to send him to school.
However, when he was 14, they seem to have changed their mind. In
Caen, the nearby city, John studied "humanities," a new type of education pioneered by the Jesuits, which included philosophy, rhetoric, and
classic literature in Latin and Greek. The focus was on being able to
understand human culture and engage civil life. At first, John was not a
brilliant student, but he was both curious and a hard worker.

Here, he also began to develop an interior life, thanks to the spiritual formation and example of his Jesuit instructors. They taught him a
way of praying that was not simply repeating set formulas, but engaging

the mind and imagination to talk with the Lord like a real person. He would ask questions in his prayer, and he would find an answer. It was an early start for a relationship, and later, in a conversation with the Blessed Mother, he would thank her for this opportunity:

"How much am I in your debt, oh Mother of Goodness, for inspiring my parents to put me under the discipline and direction of the holy Society of Jesus, in the city of Caen... being taught by Father Robin, a virtuous and pious regent who spoke about God often and with extraordinary fervor, and who helped me more than I can say in matters of salvation... It was here, oh Mother of Grace, that I received one of the greatest graces from my God, through your intervention." [4]

What was this great grace? John was a member of a Marian movement that the Jesuits had formed with a few of the students, which proposed a consecration to Mary. Deep within John's heart, something told him that this consecration was a call to imitate Mary's virginity and become a priest. It was a major decision for a 17 year-old, but he was willing to let faith and his relationship with God change his life. It is said that he slipped a ring onto the finger of Mary's statue, as a way to express this decision and ask for her help in following through on his promise.

Just a few years earlier, Madame de Sacy's mentor, Cardinal de Berulle, had founded the Oratory of Jesus and Mary in Paris. The group of priests, laity, and religious gathered around the Cardinal constituted a "silicon valley" of spirituality, a vehicle of revival in the priesthood, and a movement to spread the renewal just beginning in the city. After graduating from his Jesuit school, John decided to leave Normandy for Paris, where he could be a part of this exciting mission.

His parents were the only obstacle. They had recently tried to arrange a marriage for him, but he replied that he was already engaged to someone more beautiful, more noble, and more rich: Mary." Regardless, John's father wanted him to inherit the farm and continue his legacy, and the family stubbornness did not make discussion easy. One day, John decided it was time to leave despite his parents' opposition. He packed his bags and mounted his horse to depart; however, the animal refused to move.

It could have been just a coincidence, but John's conscience was already burning and he saw it as a communication from God. He got down from the horse, returned home, and humbly asked the permission of his father. Miraculously, permission was granted.

Chapter Three
A Disciple and Evangelist

"Son though He was, He learned
obedience through what He suffered."

— Hebrews 5:8

When St. John Eudes arrived, Paris was the scene of a major transformation. The Council of Trent had taken place in Italy 50 years earlier, but was not accepted by the bishops of France until 1615. Vincent de Paul, appalled at the contrast between the riches of Paris and the poverty of the provinces, founded his first charitable society in 1617, and laid the foundations for Church social teaching. In 1619, Francis de Sales published the *Introduction to the Devout Life,* which put forth the radical idea that it was possible for a Christian to achieve sanctity outside of a convent or monastery. It was a time of evangelical fervor, and the leaders of this renewal came to be known as the French School of Spirituality.

In 1623, John Eudes knocked on the door of the Oratory to ask Cardinal de Berulle for permission to join. Imagine the scene: a country boy from the middle of nowhere at the doorstep of a brand new church on palace grounds, right next-door to the Louvre. It seems that the cardinal was impressed by the way he presented himself because John was admitted right away and began formation as an Oratorian on March 25, six days later. Berulle would become his personal mentor and spiritual father.

The focus of Berulle's spirituality was the Incarnation. He insisted that Christ's life on earth teaches us how to live daily life as Christians.

If we really believe that, it has major implications for everything we do, especially within the Church. In Berulle's time, he saw the priesthood being sought as a way to gain power and the lucrative "benefices" that came from being a pastor, bishop or abbot. But the priest, more than anyone else, is called to imitate Christ, *"who emptied Himself, taking the form of a slave, coming in human likeness... He humbled Himself, becoming obedient to death, even death on a cross"* (Phil. 2:7-8). In His life and His death, Jesus totally poured Himself out in love for us, and every moment of His life was spent in sharing the Gospel. Therefore, a priest must do the same.

This radical call resonated deeply in John Eudes' heart. With the fiery passion of his youth and everything available to him in Paris, he could be active day and night. It was a great contrast to his little village in Normandy. Famous preachers began to draw crowds of thousands, the new movements of laity met in houses and parlors for groups of prayer, and John became involved in everything he could. He also poured himself into study of Scripture and the Church Fathers. His fervor was so great that he was even granted permission to begin preaching before he was ordained.

In 1625 (the same year John Eudes was ordained), a synod of bishops met in Paris to discuss a key issue for the church in France. The Council of Trent had ordered each diocese to establish a formation program for their priests. Up until this point, priests had no formal education, and almost all candidates were taught by following another priest around as their apprentice. In fact, the expression "hocus pocus" was coined in the years leading up to this reform, as priests with little understanding of the Latin prayers ad-libbed the words of consecration.

The suggestion of the council was to found permanent institutions called "seminaries," but as with all new ideas, the difficulty would be discovering how to make them work. Over the following century, this project would be spearheaded by the masters of the French School of Spirituality like St. Vincent de Paul, Cardinal Berulle, Jean-Jacques Olier (who founded the Sulpicians), and St. John Eudes.

The proceedings of this synod were of great interest to John Eudes, however, his ambition had already taken a toll on him. His first assignment after ordination was two years of bedrest in the sanctuary of

Aubervilliers. The most probable cause is that he had worked himself into a state of total exhaustion and needed to recuperate before he could continue his apostolic work. It must have been difficult to set aside his burning desires, humbly accept his human limits, and be obedient, but later, he came to see it as the will of God:

"The years 1625 and '26, God granted me a corporal infirmity that prevented me from exterior work. He gave me these two years to be employed in retreat, to attend to my life of prayer, to reading books of piety, and in other spiritual exercises. This time was given to me as a particular grace, for which I must eternally bless and thank His divine goodness." [5]

Chapter Four
A Missionary of Mercy

"For the mercy of God, offer yourselves
as a living sacrifice, holy and pleasing
to Him."

— Romans 12:1

Once recovered from his exhaustion, John was brought back to Paris by Berulle to continue his training as a preacher. However, the Lord had other plans for him.

As soon as John arrived, a letter came from his father with urgent news: the plague had broken out in Séez, his native diocese. Hundreds were suffering and dying alone. No priest would go near the victims, for fear of contamination. If John went to their aid, he could not only console the dying, he could provide the sacraments to strengthen their hope for eternal life. It was a dangerous mission, but a direct request. He took it to prayer, asking if this letter from his earthly father represented a call from his Father in heaven as well.

He also went to discuss it with Berulle. These souls had no one to help them, so how could he refuse? Especially if he was called to be a pastor after God's own heart, the Good Shepherd who laid down His life for His sheep. Together, they decided that he should go. John took a small portable altar and mass kit, and left as a "missionary of mercy";

a title he would use throughout his life. Sadly, this was the last advice he received from his mentor. In 1629, hardly a year later, Cardinal Berulle would die of a sudden illness.

Upon arriving in Normandy, he did everything he could to ease the sufferings of the victims, and for many, he was with them in the final moments of their life. No sooner had the plague passed in one area, it broke out in another. In 1631 it struck Caen, and John returned to the city where he attended school. Here, the sick were quarantined to a field outside the city walls, sheltered by huge barrels made for Norman cider. Rather than living in the Oratorian community which had been set up in town, John moved into this field as well, also living in a barrel. In this way, he shared the conditions of those he served and kept his brother priests from contagion.

For his first public ministry as a priest, this is not what he had originally planned. However, he believed it was the will of God. In Caen, he met others who were equally serious about following the Lord's call, but who were not priests. This had an important influence on his understanding of the Church and Christian life. One was Gaston de Renty, a young baron from the next town west. At this same time, he was responding to the same call as John Eudes, caring for plague victims at the risk of his own life. He was a layman, married, with four children, nicknamed the "Church's musketeer," or "Vincent de Paul's right arm."[6] He would later become one of John's closest friends, and his example shows that ordination is not a requirement to respond to God's call, to become a missionary of His love.

Another important character was Madame Laurence de Budos, the young abbess of the Benedictine convent who owned the field where

John lived in his barrel. She would bring meals to John Eudes' barrel during the plague, being the only one willing to risk contagion. The two soon developed a deep friendship based on a common missionary spirit. His mission was in the world, hers was in the convent. All across France, religious life was in need of reform, and the "Convent of Dames" was no exception. Lapdogs and silken slippers had become the norm, and there was more talk of jelly and jam than of prayer. She had spent 25 years trying to teach her nuns how to live a Christian life. When John Eudes appeared in her backyard, she was thrilled. He was a living example of laying aside your own interests to follow the will of God. That is the fundamental vocation that tied these three together: an abbess, a priest, and a family man.

Today, we know this concept as the "universal call to holiness." It was a major emphasis of the Vatican II council, but John Eudes significantly developed it in the 17th century. In fact, it became the cornerstone of his teaching. In a book called *The Contract of Man with God in Holy Baptism*, he says:

"Whoever bears the name Christian is obliged to follow Jesus Christ in the holiness of His life and His actions. Consequently, it is pure folly to think that only priests and religious are called to a life of sanctity." [7]

He goes on to remind us of the "terms" of this contract: both the awe-inspiring gifts that God gives us by adoption into His family and incorporation into His body, and the response that we owe Him: thanksgiving and fidelity in our daily life.

The baptismal font in Ri, where John Eudes received his call to holiness in 1601.

Chapter Five

Forming the Kingdom of Jesus

"It is no longer I who live, but Christ who
lives in me"

— Galatians 2:20

After the plague died out in Caen, John began the normal work of an
Oratorian, as a missionary in Catholic parishes. Missions were the main
vehicle of the re-evangelization of Europe in his day, and much different
than the parish missions we know today. A group of missionary priests
would be sent into a town by the bishop to preach every day for weeks,
sometimes for months. Sermons usually were given in the church, but
the missionaries would take it to the streets as well: setting up chari-
ties to care for the neglected and gathering groups of workers, children,
mothers, soldiers and other small groups for specialized catechesis.
Their aim was primarily to reach lapsed Catholics, calling them to leave

behind whatever is contrary to the Gospel, to make a good confession, receive the Eucharist, and start really living their faith.

John Eudes spent 45 years of his life in this apostolate, preaching more than 100 missions during his life, each in front of thousands of people. He was made for it, too. A contemporary describes him as:

"A little man, but with a voice that was powerful and beautiful. In preaching, he employed a great deal of emotion, an ease of expression, and a vivid and fruitful imagination full of familiar comparisons. His instructions were down to earth, easy for anyone to follow, and would always bear some kind of fruit." [8]

Another would summarize his character by saying *"He was like a lion in the pulpit, but a lamb in the confessional."* [9]

Unlike some preachers of his day, he insisted on hearing confessions personally, and spent many long hours with the penitents. He liked to say: *"The preachers beat the bushes, but it's the confessors who catch the birds."* [10] This also gave him an insight into the real struggles of the people he preached to. He also insisted on visiting families in their homes, which he called the "Domestic Church." [11] He would play with the children, listen to the parents, and teach them to pray together as a family. It was in this context, sharing the daily life of the faithful, that he wrote his first book: a small pamphlet called the *"Exercises of Piety."*

His pamphlet met a very real need, and he quickly ran out of copies. Before reprinting it, he took time to expand, to deepen certain themes, and finally produced his masterpiece in 1637, titled: *"The Life and Kingdom of Jesus in the Christian's Soul."* It explained a way to holiness for the everyday Christian, but from a new perspective that was both simple and profound. In the first chapter, he explains the foundation:

"When Christians pray, they continue and fulfill the prayer of Jesus; when they work, they continue and fulfill Jesus' work life... the same when they have a meal, or take their rest... and so on, in all other daily actions done in a Christian manner.

Now you see what Christian life is: a continuation and fulfillment of the life of Jesus. We must, therefore, be so many other 'Jesus-es' on earth, in order to continue His life and work." [12]

In the book, he proposes exercises which are "doable" for anyone: it consists of finding little prayers to say during the habitual actions of our life to remind us that Jesus did them too. Then, as we contemplate Christ in our life and actions, we can develop the same attitudes, reactions, and desires that He had during His life on earth. Soon, through our efforts and the grace that comes to us through our baptism, we can begin to say with St. Paul that *"it is no longer I who live, but Christ who lives in me."* (Gal. 2:20)

His book quickly became a "best-seller," and was republished 20 times during his lifetime. In his missions, he became known as the "wonder of his time," and crowds would come from miles around to hear him preach. He was using the mass communications media of his time. His goal was to share a very concrete way of becoming aware of Christ's presence in our everyday life, and through that awareness, enter into a relationship with Him.

He went on to develop this type of practical spirituality further in another book called the *Catechism of the Missions.* It included spiritual direction personalized for different walks of life: policemen, pharmacists, businessmen, etc.

Chapter Six

A Shepherd to the Shepherds

"Tend well the flock of God in
your midst."

— 1 Peter 5:2

In addition to his teaching on baptism and the practical spirituality in his books, God also used John Eudes to give the Church new religious communities. It began with a discovery he made during his missions, that God was calling him to serve two groups of people: priests and prostitutes.

Prostitution had become widespread in his day, and in his missions, many women involved in it came to his confessional. Listening to them, John saw that they needed more than just catechesis in order to change their life. Often they had no other way of earning money, no place to live, or were wounded on an emotional or psychological level.

Once again it was a group of souls desperately in need of mercy, but most people in the Church were afraid to get involved. The answer of society at the time was to simply put them in jail, but in John Eudes' eyes, what they needed most was love. Initially, he found some laypeople willing to take the women into their homes, but this was a heavy weight on their families and a temporary fix at best. He took it to prayer and asked the counsel of his friends in Caen. In 1641, Jean de Bernières and the Blouet de Camilly family helped him rent a house they called "the Refuge." Then Marguerite Morin stepped forward, a young woman who had a conversion during one of John's missions. She moved into the Refuge, along with two or three others, to live with the women as their full-time caretakers and friends. This initial foundation would later develop into the Sisters of Our Lady of Charity, now known as the Good Shepherd Sisters.

The call to help diocesan priests was more complex. John Eudes noticed that when he would return to a village a year or two after a mission, the life of the faithful would be no better off than when he first arrived. Upon looking deeper, he realized that the priests had no more formation than the laity, and were not equipped to maintain the progress that had begun in the missions.

St. Vincent de Paul also conducted missions at this time and had seen the same problem. His response was to give catechesis for priests every Tuesday night, but it was clear that more was needed. In 1641, John Jacques Olier, who would later found the Sulpicians, had tried to establish a seminary in Chartres, but couldn't find a way to finance the daily need for food and lodging. It was forced to close before the end of the year.

This same year, John Eudes was sent as a delegate to the Oratorian general council in Paris. Fr. Condren, the successor of Cardinal Berulle, had just died, and the council had been called to elect a new superior. Berulle had founded the Oratory for the revival of the priesthood, and Condren, in the same spirit as his predecessor, had been developing the project of a seminary. However, it seems that the new superior general was not as interested in such a risky proposition.

After this disappointing general council, John Eudes continued his missions and began giving weekly catechism for priests as well. Later in 1641, he received a surprise during a mission in Coutances, when he was asked to perform an exorcism on a woman named Marie des Vallées.

She was a very controversial figure: some said she was possessed, others called her a saint. He performed the exorcism, but her behavior was unchanged. Experts now say that she appears to have had obsessive compulsive disorder, as well as an intense mystical life. Underneath it all was a heart that deeply loved Jesus and Mary, and in her, John Eudes discovered a kindred spirit who would become one of his closest friends. Surprisingly, in this first encounter, she told him of a revelation she had heard from the Lord in prayer, that his idea to *establish [a group of priests to found a seminary] was pleasing to God, and that He Himself had inspired this idea.*[13] Perhaps difficult to believe, given the resistance of his superiors. However, providence quickly made its intentions clear.

The following year, in 1642, John received a letter from the secretary of state, Cardinal Richelieu, inviting him to Paris for a conversation. It seems that the cardinal had also noticed the need for formation, and asked if John Eudes was interested in founding a seminary. He offered letters of royal approval that would also grant a certain amount of money to pay the bills.

John returned to Caen in time for Christmas, and contemplated the crossroads before him. For whatever reason, the Oratory was not willing to support him, but the Lord's call was clear enough. He called together the six diocesan priests who had become his loyal collaborators in the missions, who had also been praying for discernment in this project. On the evening of March 24, 1643, they left Caen together on pilgrimage to *Notre Dame de la Delivrande,* a nearby Marian sanctuary. They spent the night in prayer and the following morning, after celebrating the Eucharist, founded the Congregation of Jesus and Mary. It was the

feast of the Annunciation, exactly 20 years after John Eudes joined the Oratory.

Later, John Eudes would explain this new foundation to a young seminarian: *"Remember that it is for a triple purpose that God established this Congregation in His Church: First, to provide you with the means to achieve the perfection and the holiness consonant with the ecclesiastical state.*

The second is to work at saving souls through missions and the other priestly functions, the salvation of souls being the work of the Apostles, the work of Christ Himself, a work so worthy and so divine it would seem that none can surpass it.

Nevertheless, there is one that does surpass it, namely: working for the salvation and sanctification of the clergy, which amounts to saving the saviors, directing the directors, teaching the teachers, and shepherding the shepherds." [14]

Chapter Seven

A Prophet of the Heart

"I will give you a new heart, and put my
spirit within you."

— Ezekiel 36:28

"Hail heart most holy, heart most meek, most humble, most pure, devout,
wise, and merciful. Hail most loving heart of Jesus and Mary. We offer you
our heart, we consecrate it to you, we sacrifice it, enlighten it, sanctify it,
in it live and reign now and forever." [15]

This was a prayer that John Eudes and his new community said
together every day. He composed it primarily from passages written
by Sts. Gertrude and Mathilda, two Benedictine mystics from the 13th
century. These sisters had written down their supernatural experiences
in a life of contemplation, which revolved around vivid images of the
pierced side of Christ and the blood which poured from His heart out
of love for us.

As a missionary, the image of the Heart fascinated John Eudes. For teaching, it was absolutely clear and tangible. The heart is a universal sign of love, intimacy, personality, identity... In a time when God was often seen as a distant power, by speaking about the Heart of God, he could communicate that God is love and mercy itself.

The heart was more than a catechetical tool, though. Sts. Catherine of Sienna, Gertrude the Great and John Eudes' own friend, Marie des Vallees, had all undergone an experience of a "mystical heart transplant." They each described Christ coming to them, removing their heart, and replacing it with His own. There was a tantalizing mystery here. It touched on what John taught about baptism as a call to die to ourselves in order to follow the will of God and have the same desires as Christ.

One day, he found it all summarized in one chapter of Ezekiel: *"I will sprinkle clean water upon you... and from all your idols I will cleanse you. A new heart I will give you and a new spirit I will put within you; I will take out of your flesh the heart of stone... and I will put my spirit within you"* (Ez 36:25-27). This was a biblical foundation to explain the mystical experiences in tradition. More than that, this passage summarized all the most important elements that John had received from his mentors.

In the heart of Jesus he saw the incarnation: an intimate union of divinity with humanity when the Word became flesh. Today, this mystery is expressed in a whispered prayer during the consecration: "by the mystery of this water and wine, may we come to share in the divinity of Christ, who humbled Himself to share in our humanity."

It also became clear that Mary was the first beneficiary of this "divinization" when she gave her whole heart, her entire self to Christ in the annunciation. She allowed Christ to live in her, in a very literal way. John Eudes puts it this way:

"Not only does Jesus live and remain continually in the Heart of Mary, He is Himself the heart of her Heart... Jesus, you are in her, clothing her with your qualities and perfections, inclinations and dispositions, imprinting in her a most perfect image of yourself, making her so like you that whoever sees Jesus sees Mary, and he who sees Mary beholds Jesus." [16]

This union required her "yes" at the annunciation and a continual effort throughout her life. Therefore, her heart becomes the example for all baptized Christians because Christian life requires a "heart transplant." We must die to the world and ourselves, so that we can love with the Heart of Christ, and be "little Christs" on the earth.

From this point on, the Heart became John Eudes' obsession. He gathered all the biblical references he could find, and became the first to lay out a systematic theological doctrine to explain it. In fact, at his canonization, John Eudes was given the title of "Father, Doctor and Apostle of liturgical devotion to the Hearts of Jesus and Mary" because he was the first to bring this doctrine from mysticism and monasteries into public Christian life.

The statue of St. John Eudes in St. Peter's Basilica in Rome.

He began to found societies of devotion to the Sacred Heart in every town where he conducted a mission. He wrote a handbook of devotion that outlined a way of life modeled after the Heart of Mary, which would become the rule of life for an order of lay missionaries, the third order he would eventually found. He composed a mass in honor of the union of Mary's heart to that of Jesus, which was celebrated for the first time in public on February 8th , 1648. It was in the diocese of Autun, where it would continue to be celebrated every year, and where in 1673-74, a young nun named Margaret Mary Alacoque would have her visions of the Sacred Heart. She would be asked by Jesus to spread devotion to the Sacred Heart, especially on first Fridays, and to have a mass composed in its honor. St. John Eudes had just written the first mass in honor of the Sacred Heart, and his texts were chosen to be used by the global Church for almost 300 years.

The 1670s were the beginning of a wildfire of devotion that would sweep across the world in the following century. In 1899, a spiritual daughter of St. John Eudes, Bl. Maria Droste, would ask Pope Leo XIII to dedicate the world to the Sacred Heart. In 1956, Pope Pius XII would "declare unhesitatingly that the Sacred Heart is the most effective school of the love of God... which is the foundation on which to build the kingdom of God." [17]

Devotion to the Immaculate Heart would explode onto the scene as well in 1917 when Our Lady introduced herself as the Immaculate Conception during her apparition at Fatima. Pope St. John Paul II later described how this fit into the method used by God to introduce devotion to Mary's heart: He said: "For the most part it was not until the seventeenth century that under the influence of Saint John Eudes this devotion became widespread. In our own century we see that the message of Our Lady at Fatima and the consecration of the world in 1942 to the Immaculate Heart of Mary by my predecessor Pope Pius XII... have helped us to appreciate the importance of this devotion." This shows us just how important St. John Eudes' role was as the precursor of devotion to the Two Hearts. Hearts which he always taught were inseperable.

Conclusion

Faithful to the Cross

"Since we have died with Him, we believe
we will also rise with Him."

— Romans 6:8

Although John Eudes saw great grace poured out in his life, it was not an easy path. In his depiction of the Sacred Heart, he always showed both fire and the cross, because he knew from experience that loving with the Heart of Christ implied real difficulty. He once wrote:

"Cast your eyes on a crucifix and see what Christ suffered to save souls. How can you be numbered among His members unless you conform to Him? Must a new Gospel be written for you? Do you want God to send another Messiah, one of honey and roses?" [18]

In all the projects that he pioneered, there were moments of intense trial and outright suffering. However, once he believed that a project was the will of God, he never gave up until it was accomplished.

For decades, his new foundations hung on the edge of extinction. In 1646, his spiritual daughters finally received approval from the city council to operate their house of refuge in Caen. This was the vital first step, which had to be followed by ecclesial approval. The bishop, Jacques d'Angennes, began to prepare the documents, but died before being able to sign them. This death was a major setback, because Bishop d'Angennes had been their only protector from some very influential enemies.

In fact, these enemies were primarily members of John Eudes' former community, the Oratorians. Clearly, his parting had left behind some bad blood because they began to actively oppose his projects, even publishing pamphlets full of slander against him. Whatever insults came, John Eudes accepted them calmly, and began to refer to these pro-

testers as his "benefactors." Why? Because they helped the community to grow in holiness by trying their patience.

In 1650, when a new bishop was selected to succeed Msgr. D'Angennes, these "benefactors" convinced him that John Eudes was a dangerous "innovator." An order was given that the fledgling seminary must close, and the altar in their chapel must be destroyed. Another heavy blow, especially since they had just gained legal permission to operate. However, it was not the end of the Lord's work. Just two days before the order was carried out, the bishop of Coutances asked the community to open a seminary in his diocese. The little group of 9 priests moved to the neighboring diocese to continue their work one week later, almost without interruption.

As Scripture says: *"After you have suffered a little, the God of all grace who called you to His eternal glory through Christ Jesus will Himself restore, confirm, strengthen, and establish you. To Him be dominion forever. Amen."* (1 Peter 5:10-11)

John Eudes saw the restoration, establishment and confirmation referred to in these verses. When the chapel of the seminary in Coutances was built, it became the first church dedicated to the Hearts of Jesus and Mary in history. John Eudes and his friend Marie des Vallees together laid the first stone. Just two years later, in 1652, he was allowed to re-open the seminary of Caen. The following bishop would name it the official diocesan seminary, and in 1658, 350 seminarians from across Normandy would be ordained there, all formed by John Eudes and his little community.

Our Lady of Charity also began to grow, expanding into 4 cities with the help of lay associates from the Confraternity of the Sacred Heart.

They had clearly connected to a real need in society, but the idea of nuns living in the same house as prostitutes was so radical, they received constant criticism from Church authorities. On four occasions, a priest from the tiny Eudist family was sent to Rome (usually on foot), to seek papal approval for the three Eudist institutes. However, "the usual benefactors" were well connected there as well, and continually blocked their efforts.

In 1673 everything that had been built came into dire peril. A false document was circulated in Paris, stating that John Eudes was more loyal to the pope than to the King of France. At the time, this was one of the most dangerous political hotbuttons, which had recently led to people being executed. John Eudes was in Paris at the time, preaching a mission, and was advised to quickly leave town and never return. He spent six years in royal disgrace, which could at any time have become not only a danger to his life, but the destruction of all he had worked for.

John Eudes lived a long life of trial and hard work, all for the love of God. It was a continual exercise of setting aside his own will to cling to God's will. He outlived all his closest friends, and kept working and preaching until he was almost 80 years old.

At the end of 1678, he was present at the first general assembly of his Congregation of priests, called to elect his successor. The son of his closest friends, Fr. Jacques Blouet de Camilly was elected. In a touching scene, the venerable missionary asked to be brought to the young priest. He slowly lowered himself to his knees, and vowed obedience to his superior for the rest of his life. A few weeks later, he died peacefully after receiving the Eucharist, with the praise of Jesus and Mary on his lips as his final words.

He had once written: *"Lord, may my entire life be a perpetual sacrifice of love and praise for you. May my last breath be an act of purest love for you."* [19]

Did the Lord grant him this prayer? Yes. He left us a brilliantly shining example of a priest, a missionary, and a baptized Christian, whose heart was on fire with love for God and for His people, especially those most in need of mercy.

His entire life was driven by the desire to unite his heart to the Heart of Christ as completely as Our Blessed Mother did. In depictions today, he is shown with a heart in his hand, because this great Heart loved too deeply to be kept in his chest. This love is the fire that propelled him out into mission. If we allow ourselves, we too can be caught up into this furnace of merciful love that longs to consume the world. *"I have come to set the world on fire, and how I wish it was already burning."*

Jesus giving His heart to St. John Eudes, just like Mary gave her heart to Jesus. Painted in the church that once held the saint's tomb, in Caen, France.

About the Eudist Family

During his lifetime, St. John Eudes' missionary activity had three major areas of focus.

- For priests, he provided formation, education, and the spiritual support which is crucial for their role in God's plan of salvation.
- For prostitutes and others on the margins of society, he gave them a home and bound their wounds, like the Good Shepherd with his lost sheep.
- For the laity, he preached the dignity of their baptism and their responsibility to be the hands and feet of God, to continue the Incarnation.

In everything he did, he burned with the desire to be a living example of the love and mercy of God.

These are the "family values" which continue to inspire those who continue his work. To paraphrase St. Paul, John Eudes planted seeds, which others watered through the institutions he founded, and God gave the growth. Today, the family tree continues to bear fruit:

The *Congregation of Jesus and Mary* (CJM), also known as The Eudists, continues the effort to form and care for priests and other leaders within the Church. St. John Eudes called this the mission of "teaching the teachers, shepherding the shepherds, and enlightening those who are the light of the world." Continuing his efforts as a missionary preacher, Eudist priests and brothers "audaciously seek to open up new avenues for evangelization," through television, radio, and new media.

The *Religious of the Good Shepherd* (RGS) continue outreach to women in difficult situations, providing them with a deeply needed place of refuge and healing while they seek a new life. St. Mary Euphrasia drastically expanded the reach of this mission which now operates in over 70 countries worldwide. A true heiress of St. John Eudes, St. Mary Euphrasia exhorted her sisters: "We must go after the lost sheep with no other rest than the cross, no other consolation than work, and no other thirst than for justice."

In every seminary and House of Refuge founded by St. John Eudes, he also established a *Confraternity of the Holy Heart of Jesus and Mary* for the laity, now known as the Eudist Associates. The mission he gave them was twofold: First, "To glorify the divine Hearts of Jesus and Mary... working to make them live and reign in their own heart through diligent imitation of their virtues." Second, "To work for the salvation of souls... by practicing, according to their abilities, works of charity and mercy and by attaining numerous graces through prayer for the clergy and other apostolic laborers."

The *Little Sisters of the Poor* were an outgrowth of this confraternity. St. Jeanne Jugan was formed as a consecrated woman within the Eudist Family. She discovered the great need for love and mercy among the poor and elderly and the mission took on a life of its own. She passed on to them the Eudist intuition that the poor are not simply recipients of charity, they provide an encounter with Charity Himself: "My little ones, never forget that the poor are Our Lord... In serving the aged, it is He Himself whom you are serving."

A more recent "sprout" on the tree was founded by Mother Antonia Brenner in Tijuana, Mexico. After raising her children in Beverly Hills and suffering through divorce, she followed God's call to become a live-in prison minister at the *La Mesa* penitentiary. The *Eudist Servants of the*

11th Hour was founded so that other women in the latter part of their lives could imitate her in "being love" to those most in need.

The example St. John Eudes set for living out the Gospel has inspired many more individuals and organizations throughout the world. For more information about the Eudist family, news on upcoming publications, or for ways to share in our mission, contact us at spirituality@eudistsusa.org.

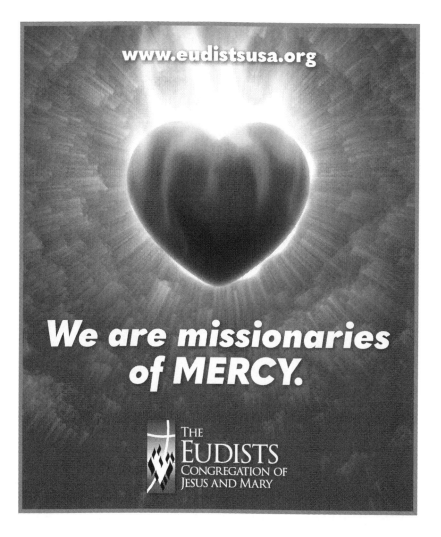

References

Introduction — A Heart on Fire

1. Charles LeBrun. *The Spiritual Teaching of St. John Eudes*. London: Sands & Co. (1934), p. 253.

Chapter One — An Adorer of Truth

2. John Eudes. "Memorial Beneficiorum Deum." *Letters and Shorter Works*. New York: P.J. Kennedy (1948), p.227-228.
3. Ibid. p. 289.

Chapter Two — A Lover of Jesus and Mary

4. John Eudes. *Letters and Shorter Works*, p. 289, 333.

Chapter Three — A Disciple and Evangelist

5. John Eudes. *Letters and Shorter Works*, p. 291.

Chapter Four — A Missionary of Mercy

6. Triboulet, Raymond. "St. Jean Eudes et Gaston de Renty," *Cahiers Eudistes* #17, Rome: Eudist General House (1995), p. 13-23.
7. Robert dePas. *Life, to Me, is Christ: St. John Eudes and His Message*. Barcelona: Editorial Claret (2001), p. 50. N.B. The *Contract* cited was translated into English in 1869 by a diocesan priest and reprinted by Loretto Publications in 2012 with minimal changes. However, the translator seems to have left out significant sections of the original work, including our quote. It can be found in French, in John Eudes' *Oevres Completes* II, Paris: Beauchesne (1906), p. 222.

Chapter Five — Forming the Kingdom of Jesus

8. Paul Milcent. *Jean Eudes, Artisan du Renouveau Chretien au XVIIe Siecle*, p. 49. In English, cf. A. Pinas. *The Venerable Pere Eudes and His Works: 1601-1901*. Edinburgh: T & A Constable (1903), p. 141.

9. Milcent, p. 469. Cf. also Pinas, p. 139.

10. Milcent, p. 50. Cf. also Pinas, p. 138.

11. Milcent, p. 214.

12. John Eudes. *The Life and Kingdom of Jesus,* New York: P.J. Kennedy (1947), p. 6.

Chapter Six — A Shepherd to the Shepherds

13. Milcent, p. 98.

14. Clement Guillon. *In All Things, the Will of God: St. John Eudes Through His Letters.* Buffalo, NY: St. John Eudes Center (1994), p. 79.

Chapter Seven — A Prophet of the Heart

15. John Eudes. "Heart of the Holy Family A Eudist Manual of Prayer." *Eudist Prayer Books.* Los Angeles, CA: Heart of Home (2014). Ebook available on Amazon.com

16. John Eudes, *The Admirable Heart of Mary,* New York: P.J. Kennedy (1948), p. 53. Also *The Kingdom of Jesus,* p. 204.

17. Pope Pius XII, *Haurietis Aquas — Encyclical letter,* 1956, #123.

Conclusion — Faithful to the Cross

18. Guillon, p. 68.

19. John Eudes. "Letter to the Most Holy Virgin." *Letters and Shorter Works,* p. 324.

About the Author

Steven S. Marshall is a specialist in the spiritual heritage of St. John Eudes. He blogs (doctorcordis.com) about spirituality and his collaboration with the Vatican commission evaluating St. John Eudes as a candidate to be proclaimed a Doctor of the Church.

Steven S. Marshall

He holds a MA in Spiritual Theology from St. John's Seminary. Highest honors were awarded to his thesis: "Eudist Brothers: Living Communion Ecclesiology 'Before it was Cool.'" For a year he lived in Normandy, France as one of 15 people in a specialized program of spirituality studies. There, he walked in the footsteps of St. John Eudes and sat at the feet of spiritual masters from around the world. He now serves as translator and theologian for the US Region of the Eudists and lives with his wife in Southern California.

Made in the USA
Columbia, SC
08 July 2018